Hound in the Hi

World famous c
and his faithful co
ing the unhappy
matchless pedigre
an ancient curse –
bagpipes very badly
Sporrans? His efforts ious and
exciting reading.

Brenda Sivers was born in England but has lived in France, Africa and Canada. She has been a journalist and magazine editor and has now returned to England to live in the West Country, where she works as a public relations officer. Her other exciting adventure of Sherlock Hound, *Hound and the Witching Affair*, is also published by Beavers.

THE ADVENTURES OF SHERLOCK HOUND

HOUND IN THE HIGHLANDS

Brenda Sivers

Illustrated by Frank Rodgers

Beaver Books

First published in 1980 by Abelard-Schuman
Limited, A Member of the Blackie Group, Furnival
House, 14–18 High Holborn, London WC1V 6BX

This paperback edition published in 1981 by
The Hamlyn Publishing Group Limited
London · New York · Sydney · Toronto
Astronaut House, Feltham, Middlesex, England
(Paperback Division: Hamlyn Paperbacks,
Banda House, Cambridge Grove,
Hammersmith, London W6 0LE)

ISBN 0 600 20360 3

Printed and bound in Great Britain by
Cox & Wyman Limited, Reading

Contents

For Alan, with love

1

Oatcakes, Bannocks and Bridies

"How much further, Hound?" said Winston in a weak voice.

"Less than a mile, I assure you," said the bloodhound, "and pray keep yourself well covered," he added, draping another blanket over Dr Winston's sagging shoulders. "This damp Scottish air is most harmful to the health."

"I know," agreed Winston, burying his watery eyes and runny nose in a large spotted handkerchief. "And the trouble is I can't stop . . . I . . . c . . . c . . . c . . . c . . . c . . . c . . . can't stop . . . achoo-oooooooooooing!" And he let out such a sneeze that the coach horses shied and whinnied.

"Do not despair," said Hound soothingly. "My brother's housekeeper, the excellent Mrs MacDougall, will take good care of you. I fancy a hot bath and an even hotter drink will soon have you as right as rain."

Winston groaned. "Oh, I do wish you hadn't used that word," he said. "It hasn't stopped raining since we came to the Highlands." And he looked forlornly at the torrent of water pouring continuously from the grey skies, drenching everything and everyone.

"Ay," said the coachman, butting into the conversation. "This weather's nae guid for man or beast. I canna think wha's happened to yon sun."

"It's gone to a warmer place," muttered Winston, "and I wish I'd gone with it." He turned to the bloodhound sitting beside him. "Hound," he asked, lowering his voice so as not to offend the coach driver, "why does your brother live in such a cold, wet part of the country?"

"My brother Shylock married a Scottish lady of considerable wealth," explained the bloodhound, "and since country life appeals to him, he decided to leave London, the city of his noble birth, and live in Glen Kelpie in the ancestral home of his wife's family."

"Uhm," grunted Winston. "He may be your brother but he doesn't sound much like you."

"Indeed he is not," agreed Sherlock Hound. "There is a strong physical likeness, of course, since we are identical twins, but our temperaments are quite different. However, I would hasten to point out that you are seeing Glen Kelpie in its worst light..." he paused. "Indeed, in this heavy mist, you are hardly seeing it in any light. I assure you that in the summer, it is an exceedingly pleasant place."

"Hound," sighed Winston, "this *is* the summer."

"What? Oh . . . oh yes. I had quite forgotten."

"That's understandable," shivered Winston,

as a strong gust of icy wind rocked the coach from side to side. "Tell me, what does your brother Shylock do?"

Hound smiled. "In his own way, he is quite a detective."

Winston raised his eyebrows in surprise, but since his face was half covered with a shaggy fringe of hair, the expression was lost on his companion.

"Just as I track down criminals," explained Hound, "so my brother tracks down antiques . . . rare and beautiful things that belong to the past. Indeed, apart from brotherly affection, the reason for my present visit is to view a particularly fine clarsach which has recently come into Shylock's possession. You are familiar, of course, with the Scottish clarsach?"

"Oh, of course," said Winston stoutly. "How very interesting, a clarsach," he murmured. "Yes, very interesting indeed."

"Where did you have the opportunity of seeing one?" enquired Hound.

Winston shifted uncomfortably under his mound of blankets. "Well, I can't exactly remember where," he said, turning red in the face, "in fact I might say . . . ah . . . I might say . . . ah . . . ah . . . ah . . ."

"Look to your horses!" Hound shouted to the coachman.

" . . . ah . . . ah . . . achoooooooooooooooo!" sneezed Winston.

"I suggest you say nothing more until we arrive safely at Kelpie Hall," said Hound, a touch sarcastically. "Another sneeze like that and the horses will bolt."

Soon they turned through wrought-iron double gates and drove up a long, tree-lined path at the end of which stood an impressive stone house. As the coach neared the house, the front door suddenly opened and out sprang a bloodhound.

Winston started. "Good heavens!" he cried. "Why it's . . ."

"My brother," chuckled Sherlock. "I told you we were identical twins."

"Sherlock!"

"Shylock!"

The two brothers embraced warmly.

"Allow me to present to you my friend and colleague Dr Winston," said Hound, turning to the sheepdog huddled in a corner of the coach.

"Delighted to make your acquaintance," said Shylock Hound, extending a paw.

"It's a ple . . . a ple . . . a ple . . . " replied Winston.

"A what?" frowned Shylock Hound, quite confused.

"Stand back, Shylock!" barked Hound urgently, pulling his brother to safety.

"A ple . . . a plechoooooooooooooooooo!"

"Poor Winston has contracted a rather severe cold in this northerly climate," explained Hound, as the three of them entered the house.

"Have you been in Scotland long then?" said his brother, showing them into a comfortable sitting room.

"A week or so," replied Hound. "I have been in Inverness solving a rather interesting little case. It concerned a certain chieftain of the Clan MacGregor who tossed the caber some fifty yards at the Highland Games."

His brother looked puzzled. "But there's nothing criminal in that," he protested.

"Unfortunately," retorted Hound drily, "he tossed the caber on to the head of the chieftain of the Clan Campbell."

"Ah yes, I do remember reading something about that in the *Kelpie Chronicle*," said Shylock. "Sit here, Dr Winston." He turned to the sheepdog, who looked like a walking blanket shop, and pointed to a comfortable armchair in front of the peat fire.

"Move over, Spot! Out of the way, Rover!" he commanded, kicking a couple of guinea pigs who were roasting their rumps in the flames.

The Hound brothers made themselves comfortable on the settee and chatted about family affairs while Dr Winston snuffled and sneezed in his corner. He was quite fascinated by the startling resemblance between the two bloodhounds. They had the same long, dangling ears, sad, bloodshot eyes and soft golden fur. Even their voices were of the same low, rather gruff pitch, their speech slow and drawling. Shylock bit his claws and tapped restlessly on the table while he talked . . . just like Sherlock. And Sherlock laughed in a hearty, yet strangely noiseless fashion . . . just like Shylock.

After a while, the door opened and a plump little Skye terrier waddled in carrying an enormous tray loaded with cucumber sandwiches, scones and strawberry jam, chocolate cake and ginger biscuits, which she placed on the table.

Winston's eyes lit up. "Ah!" he exclaimed. "Real English t . . . t . . . t . . . "

The housekeeper backed away, alarmed.

"T . . . t . . . tachooooooooooooooooooooo!"

"I think he was trying to say 'real English tea'," explained Hound, helping the Skye terrier to her paws. "With all due respect to your country's cooking, Mrs MacDougall, my colleague does not care for oatcakes, bannocks and bridies."

"The poor wee laddie has a rare cold," said the housekeeper, looking at Winston in a motherly fashion. "And I've just the cure for it," she added.

"Lemon and honey?" said Winston hopefully.

She shook her head. "Nay, lad. I'm goin' to give ye a big dish o' Carrageen Jelly."

Winston looked doubtful.

"Carrageen Jelly?" he said.

"Ay. It's my mother's recipe. It's made from dried seaweed and milk."

Winston, who had been about to bite into a

thick slice of chocolate cake, slapped a napkin to his mouth and turned a bilious shade of green. For some reason, he refused to eat anything more that day, even turning down his favourite ginger snaps.

After tea, Shylock Hound rose to his paws and left the room. He returned within minutes bearing a small silver harp encrusted with crystals.

"Ah," said Sherlock, reaching for it eagerly. "What a little beauty!"

"It belonged to a cousin of my late wife," explained Shylock, trying not to wince as his brother plucked a few flat chords. "But if you wish to see some truly magnificent examples of the Highland harp, I suggest you pay a visit to MacSporran of MacSporran, chief of the MacSporran clan on the Isle of Bogles. He is a splendid fellow, descended directly from the Lords of the Isles, and he has harps in his possession that date back to Robert the Bruce."

Hound's whiskers twitched with excitement. "Is the Isle of Bogles far from here?" he asked.

"Just over the water," replied his brother. "One of the lobster fishermen will take you in his boat and I will give you a letter of introduction to the MacSporran. You'll enjoy meeting him, I know. He's a charming fellow."

Hound turned to Winston. "Do you feel up to it?" he enquired.

Winston sneezed loudly by way of answer.

"I think you should let Dr Winston rest for a

few days," suggested Shylock in a kindly fashion. "A warm bed and the occasional hot toddy should return the fellow to full health."

"For my part," said Hound, "I think a good dose of Mrs MacDougall's Carrageen Jelly will have him on his paws in no time."

"Uh . . . when are we going to see the clarsach?" cut in Winston, anxious to change the subject as quickly as possible.

Hound held up the small silver harp. "This is the clarsach," he said, trying not to laugh.

"Oh . . . oh yes, of course it is. Silly of me," said Winston, beside himself with embarrassment. "I just couldn't see without my glasses."

"But you don't wear glasses," protested Hound.

"No, but I should," retorted Winston. "And now, if you will excuse me, I will go up to my room," he said, rising to his paws. "Gentlemen, I bid you both goodn . . . goodn . . . n . . . n . . ."

The two guinea pigs scampered under the settee and clamped their paws over their ears.

"Goodn . . . nachoooooooooooooooooooooo!" sneezed Winston. And left the room.

2

The Isle of Bogles

Within a few days, Winston was well again. Though Mrs MacDougall had made him a hearty helping of Carrageen Jelly, he refused point blank to touch it, bolting his door against her until she promised to return with more appetising food, like suet pudding with treacle and spotted dick with custard.

From the lower quarters of the house he heard a continual tuneless twanging which he took to be Hound torturing the brass strings of the Highland harp. This was confirmed by the appearance of Mrs MacDougall in a large bonnet pulled firmly over her ears and Shylock in ear muffs. Both were clearly relieved when Hound and Winston declared their intention of leaving for the Isle of Bogles and I have it on good authority that the harp itself was thrown into the nearest lake, the master of the house declaring he couldn't bear to look at the wretched thing any more.

The day of their departure dawned dull and overcast with the threat of rain in the air. The fisherman who was to row them over to the Isle of

Bogles was waiting patiently by his little dory, which pitched and tossed in the choppy waters. Though the crossing was no more than an hour or so, Mrs MacDougall had thoughtfully prepared a picnic hamper of cold beef, pheasant sandwiches, apple pie and cinnamon biscuits. Before tucking into the feast, however, Dr Winston searched the basket carefully until he found what he was looking for.

In the very bottom left hand corner was tucked a small bowl containing a greenish jelly. With his paw clamped firmly over his nose, the sheepdog tipped the contents of the bowl into the ocean. Immediately a seal, which had followed them closely for several miles, swam quickly to the side of the boat and swallowed the jelly in one gulp.

"I wonder if he enjoyed it," said Winston, looking at the creature intently.

"I rather think not," said Hound. "Indeed, the Carrageen Jelly appears to have made him decidedly ill."

The seal had clapped a flipper to its mouth and was making frantic gestures to Dr Winston.

"What do you think he wants?" asked the sheepdog anxiously.

"It is really quite obvious what the poor fellow wants," said Hound. "He is in urgent need of a rather large paper bag."

"Oh yes, of course," agreed Winston, diving back into the picnic hamper.

"Here's one," he said, throwing it to the seal. "Oh well caught, Sir!" he shouted.

The seal acknowledged the compliment with a wave of its flipper and then swam quickly away, its nose buried deeply in the paper bag.

"And now for lunch," said Winston, tucking into a juicy beef bone.

"Can I interest you in a cucumber sandwich?" he said politely to the fisherman, a perky little Scottish terrier by the name of Jamie.

The fisherman sniffed disdainfully at the feast spread before him.

"Sassenach food!" He grunted in disgust. "Give me a guid haggis or a black puddin'," he said. "But I'll nae touch that stuff."

"That 'stuff' as you call it, my good man," snapped Winston indignantly, "is . . . yeouw!" And he let out a howl of agony.

"I don't care what you call it, mon," said Jamie, "though 'yeouw' is as guid a name as any."

"That isn't its name, you fool!" exclaimed Winston angrily. "I said 'yeouw' because something has just bitten my toe." And he held up a paw from which dangled a large lobster.

"Hey! Yon's one of mine!" protested the fisherman.

"I don't care whose lobster it is," retorted Winston.

"Weel, I'm afeered there'll be a wee charge for him, Sir."

"But I don't want him," protested Winston hotly.

"Nae, but he seems to want ye."

"Then let *him* pay!" snapped Winston.

The fisherman thought this over carefully. "Na, that's nae guid," he said finally. "He hasna a penny to bless hisself with. Duncan!" he barked. "Get back under yon seat where ye belong."

The lobster obediently dropped off Winston's paw, smiled apologetically, and crawled away.

The rest of the crossing passed uneventfully and soon the gaunt black cliffs of the Isle of Bogles came into view.

"Ye'll be stayin' with the MacSporran, nae doot," said the fisherman.

Hound nodded.

"Weel, that's his castle yonder," and he pointed to a grim fortress perched atop the cliffs. "It's called Castle Bogle, after the island."

"Bogle," repeated Winston. "Bogle. Does that mean anything?"

"Ay, it does, laddie," nodded Jamie. "It's the Gaelic for ghost."

Winston's jaw dropped open.

"Ghost!" he repeated in horror, as if he had just seen one.

"Ay, laddie, ghost," insisted the fisherman. "Yon castle's been haunted for many a year. They say a fearful phantom appears at midnight, gnashin' its teeth and wailin' like a banshee."

"A . . . b . . . b . . . banshee?" exclaimed Winston,

his teeth chattering like monkeys. "What's a banshee?"

"I couldna say," the fisherman shook his head, "I'm only repeatin' the story as I heard it."

"You are only repeating stuff and nonsense, my good man," said Hound tartly, as he stepped ashore. "Come, Winston. We must be on our way."

"If ye need me," said Jamie, rowing quickly away from the dreaded island, "ye must light a rocket. When I see it, I'll come to fetch ye."

"But where will we get a rocket?" asked Winston.

"Ye can buy them on the mainland," replied the fisherman.

"Oh good," said the sheepdog, turning to follow Hound up the long steep road to the castle. Then he stopped.

"But how will we get back to the mainland to buy one?" he asked.

"That's your problem," answered Jamie. And he rowed away.

3

The Curse of the MacSporrans

MacSporran of MacSporran was a Scottish deerhound descended from a long line of noble dogs. He towered over Winston and Hound, a magnificent figure in his brown short coat and waistcoat with gold buttons, a kilt in the clan tartan and matching stockings. A huge plaid was thrown over his shoulders and on his head he wore a blue bonnet with a dogberry, the MacSporran badge, and three feathers to show he was a clan chief.

"*Ceud mile failte*," he said, when he met the two visitors. "A hundred thousand welcomes. Do you have the Gaelic, my friends?"

Hound shook his head. "Alas no," he said. "Although I bark fifteen languages fluently, Gaelic is not one of them. I must remember to learn it one day when I have a moment."

"You are welcome to Castle Bogle," said the chief, "and you must stay as long as you wish."

"Where's the gho . . . ?" began Winston.

"I understand from my brother," said Hound, interrupting Winston abruptly, "that you have a magnificent collection of Highland harps in your possession."

"Indeed I do," nodded the chief, "and I shall be delighted to show them to you after lunch. In the meantime, Jock will take you to your rooms."

He turned to an old and greying Scottish terrier, leaning heavily on a gnarled cane.

"Are the guest quarters ready, Jock?" he enquired.

"Och ay," said the terrier, touching his bonnet with his paw. "All's ready and prepared. Follow me, gentlemen," and he led Hound and Winston out of the great hall of the castle.

By Winston's reckoning, they walked at least five miles, through long, cold passageways and up winding stone stairs, finally coming to a halt in front of a stout wooden door.

"Yon's the quarters for distinguished guests," said Jock, turning a gigantic key in the lock.

"Are they haunt . . . ?" began Winston.

"Thank you, my good man," interrupted Hound, brushing past the other two dogs and entering the huge room. "Splendid," he said, his eyes lighting up at the sight of the great canopied bed and the rich tapestries that decorated the walls. "I must confess this is the first real castle I have ever slept in. The castles of England so often lack a real feeling of age, whereas this . . ." he raised his paws in admiration, "one can almost feel the generations of MacSporrans who have lived in this noble building."

"Ay," agreed the terrier drily, "and sometimes ye can see and hear them too."

Winston's fur stood on end. "You d . . . don't mean?" he stammered.

"Ay, laddie, I do," said Jock. "I'm talkin' o' wee ghosties. But I'll let ye find out for yourselves," he added, turning to leave. "If there's anythin' ye'll be needin', just let me know."

"Oh there is, there is," said Winston hastily.

"Ay?"

"Would you book me a room in the local inn? I find the air in this castle too damp for my lungs. I suffer from bronchitis, you know," he added, coughing painfully to prove his point.

But the terrier only laughed in a dour way. "There's nae inn on the Isle of Bogles, mon," he said. "You must stay in the castle, or sleep on the beach."

"We shall be very pleased to stay in the castle," cut in Hound icily, "but I should be grateful, my good fellow, if you would indicate the direction of the nearest post office."

Again the terrier laughed. "There's nae post office on this island, laddie. Nae doctor. And nae constable either. A lobster boat comes over once a week, if the weather's guid. And that's our only communication wi' the mainland."

Winston fell in a heap on the nearest chair.

"Lunch is at two o'clock," continued Jock. "The dining room's in the West Wing. Gae doon these stairs, turn left, right, left, right, through the main hall, up the spiral staircase, along the gallery, past the gun room, round the library and ye're there. Ye'll have nae trooble findin' it. Good day, gentlemen." And he left.

"We've simple fare for lunch," said the MacSporran when they entered the huge oak-panelled dining room some time later. "Pickled herrings followed by hotch-potch and crowdie."

"I think I'll just have a roll and butter, thank you," said Winston, taking his place at the great table.

The chief laughed. "Have no fear," he said, "hotch-potch is stew, a dish, I think, you Sassenachs enjoy as much as we Highlanders. And crowdie is a very tasty cheese."

Winston was relieved. As he ate, he stole quick glances at the MacSporran who was, without doubt, one of the finest dogs he had ever seen. Despite his great size and evident strength, the clan chief had a quiet grace and dignity about him which, combined with the soft burr of his speech, completely enchanted the Old English sheepdog. Hound too was obviously charmed by the chief, questioning him closely about the ancient line of Scottish deerhounds, which could be traced back to the Middle Ages. The MacSporran chatted amiably but, after a time, Winston noticed a certain sadness in his eyes and a nervous twitch of his tail which suggested some inner tension.

"My young nephew lives here with me," he

said, as the meal drew to an end. "You will have the pleasure of meeting him this evening at dinner."

"You have no family of your own?" enquired Hound.

The MacSporran shook his head. "I shall be . . ." he hesitated and then corrected himself, "I was going to be married at the end of this month," a sorrowful look had come back to his eyes, "but I don't think the wedding will take place after all . . ." His voice faded away.

Hound and Winston waited for him to continue but he stayed silent, lost in a daydream.

"If you have no sons," persisted Hound, who liked to get at the facts, "the castle and its estates will go to your nephew when you die, I suppose?"

"Ay," nodded the chief. "He is my dead brother's only son, the last of the line. After him, there are no more MacSporrans."

And he lapsed into a brooding silence.

When several minutes had gone by, Winston coughed discreetly. The chief came back to earth with a start.

"My apologies, gentlemen," he said. "My mind is rather troubled of late but I should not burden my guests with my worries. Mr Hound, if you will come with me I shall be most happy to show you my collection of clarsachs."

Hound followed the chief eagerly, while Winston wandered off for a tour of the castle and grounds. After his recent embarrassment over clarsachs, he had no wish to get involved with the wretched things again.

The castle was cold and damp and ominous. Winston crept stealthily through its dark, draughty corridors, pausing now and again to examine some ancient shield or sword, until he came to a door which led into a garden, and since the sun was attempting to shine, he stepped out. At the end of the garden was a maze, a network of passages between tall hedges designed to confuse anyone who dared enter.

Winston approached it confidently, glad to have found something to take his mind off the gloom of the haunted castle, if only for a short while. "It's probably only a very small maze," he told himself, trotting up one path and down the next. "I shall soon be out of it."

But when he thought he should be coming out the other side, he was astonished to discover he was still somewhere in the middle. So he set out again, this time with a little less bravado. Round and round he went, growing more and more desperate as he turned each corner to meet yet another dead end.

"Bother," he said loudly . . . and set off again.

He was beginning to get hot under the collar and to feel not a little foolish. He had visions of going round and round in the abominable maze for ever, his body growing thinner and thinner, his mind more confused, until he dropped in a lifeless heap to the ground, never to be seen or heard of until somebody found him years later, a pile of white, brittle bones.

He began to sweat and, in a moment of sheer panic, he let out a howl of fear. "Help! Help!" he cried.

"Och ay!" said a voice close by.

Winston leaped into the air. "Who . . . ?" He turned quickly. But nobody was there. He doubled back along the path and rounded the corner . . . but still could not see anybody.

"Who's there?" he said.

"Me," said a voice a few feet from his ear.

"Me?" repeated Winston.

"Ay. Me," returned the voice, quite sure of itself.

Suddenly a terrible thought sprang into the sheepdog's mind. Since the voice appeared to have no body, could it be . . . could it possibly belong to the fearful ghost the fisherman had told him about? Had it followed him from the castle into this dreadful maze? Was it dogging his steps, waiting for him to drop exhausted. Would it leap upon him, when he was too weak to resist, and . . . ?

Winston let out a howl of terror and backed into a hedge, getting horribly tangled in branches and twigs.

"Help!" he whimpered. "Help!"

"Dinna take on so, laddie," rasped the same voice, "I'm just round the corner from ye."

With relief, Winston recognised it as the gruff voice of Jock.

Sure enough, the old dog was lazing in the hedgerow, a pillow under his head and a bottle of Scotch close to paw.

"It's the only place for a wee spot o' peace and quiet," he explained. "Until you came crashin' along," he added ruefully. "Here, mon, take a swig o' this." He offered Winston the bottle. "Ye look more in need of it than I do."

"I'm quite all right, really," said Winston, putting his paws behind his back so the other dog couldn't see them shaking. "I just got a little lost."

"Ye canna be a little lost, mon," said Jock, precisely. "Ye're either lost . . . or ye're not."

The sheepdog shuffled from one paw to the other.

"Weel, sit down now ye're here, laddie," suggested Jock, "and we'll have a wee blether."

"I'd rather not drink, thank you," said Winston.

"Tch!" The Scot shook his head irritably. "A blether's a chat, mon, not a tot o' whisky. Sit here," he patted a soft pile of earth next to him, "and tell me what ye and yon bloodhound want wi' the MacSporran."

"Mr Hound has a keen interest in clarsachs," explained Winston, "and since your master has a fine collection . . ."

"Och ay, that he has," interrupted Jock. "Some o' the best ye'll ever see . . . and all encrusted with precious gems. Does yon Hound play the harp then?"

"In a manner of speaking," Winston chose his words carefully, "I suppose one could say that he does."

The Scot looked at him in disgust. "Can you Sassenachs nae give a simple answer to a simple question?" he demanded. "Can he play the harp. Ay or nae?"

"Nae," muttered Winston, feeling, despite his honesty, that he had somehow betrayed Hound.

"Weel, the MacSporran can," said Jock, taking another swig from the whisky bottle. "He plays like an angel at the pearly gates."

"Maybe we shall hear him," said Winston.

"Ay," the Scot nodded his head. "Ye'll hear him right enough. That's all he does these days, poor mon. Shuts hisself up in his room and plays mournful tunes on the harp, from noon till night."

"Is something wrong with him then?"

"Ay, laddie, somethin's very wrong. The curse o' the MacSporrans is on him."

Winston's ears pricked up. "The curse?"

"Have ye nae heard of it, mon?" said Jock in surprise. "I had nae idea ye Sassenachs were sae ignorant. Ay, there is a curse on this house and I'll tell ye how it came aboot." He put a paw round Winston's shoulders and drew him closer. "Many years ago, the MacSporran's great-great-great-great-great-grandfather . . . or was it his great-great-great-great-grandfather?" He paused to consider this while Winston fidgeted impatiently. "Nae, it was his great-great-great-

great-great-grandfather who killed the castle piper," Jock decided at last. "And terrible it was . . . the piper's playin', I mean. The chief's ears were so sorely tried by it, he flew into a rage one night, took the leather bag o' the pipes between his great paws and pressed hard, thereby forcin' all the air back into the piper, who swelled up like a balloon and exploded, several parts of him landin' on surroundin' islands."

"Horrible!" shuddered Winston.

"Ay, that it was," agreed Jock. "But ye see he'd never had a lesson in his life and the pipes are nae easy to play."

"I was talking about the piper's death, not his playing," snapped Winston.

"Since that terrible night," continued Jock, "the poor piper's ghost has haunted the castle, moanin' and wailin' all night long and puttin' the fear o' God into all who hear him. Nae pipes are allowed on the island on pain o' death, but ye'll hear them now right enough. Ye'll hear them tonight," he said, "and every night until the MacSporran dies."

"Dies?" echoed Winston. "Is he sick then?"

"Ay, lad, sick with fear. For when the wee ghostie starts to play his pipes, it means the curse has come again to the Hoose o' MacSporran and the chief will die a dreadful death within the month."

"How awful!" whispered Winston.

"It is," agreed Jock. "And keeps me awake all

night long. But the poor laddie's never had a lesson in his life, ye see, and the pipes are nae easy to . . ."

"I was talking about the curse," said Winston irritably.

"The MacSporran was to be married to a bonnie wee lass, daughter of a chieftain from the Isle o' Skye," continued Jock, "but he'll nae see his wedding day, I'm afeered."

Winston shook his head sadly. "Poor man," he sighed.

"Ay," agreed the Scot, "he doesna stand a dog's chance."

"Did all his ancestors die because of the curse?" said Winston, his flesh beginning to creep at the very thought.

"Every one," said Jock. "Dreadful, dreadful deaths."

"Oh, don't tell me," protested Winston, covering his ears.

"Och weel, I won't then," said the Scot matter of factly.

"Well, you could just briefly dcscribc one or two of the less gruesome ones," suggested the sheepdog.

"Weel, there was Angus, the present MacSporran's great-grandfather. He choked to death on a bowl of porridge."

"Choked on porridge?" exclaimed Winston. "But that's not possible."

"Ay, it is. At least it is the way his wee wife

made it," said Jock. "There were lumps in it as big as golf balls, they say. And then there was Alisdair. He got drunk one night and stepped out on to the balcony for a breath o' fresh air."

"But what's dangerous about that?" said Winston.

"The castle doesna have a balcony," explained Jock drily. "And then there was Dugald. He was bitten to death by his own sporran . . ."

"Stop!" Winston held up a paw. "I can't stand any more. Is there nothing that can be done for the MacSporran to save him from a similar tragedy?"

"Nae, laddie. Wherever he goes, the curse will surely dog his steps."

"So his nephew will inherit the castle?"

"Dinna blether to me about his nephew," snapped Jock. "It was a bad day for us all when that one came to Castle Bogle. He fancies he's the chief already. But the MacSporran's nae dead yet."

"What's wrong with the young man?" asked Winston.

"Wrong? Wrong?" The old Scot hooted in scorn. "It would take less time to tell ye wha's right with him," he barked, pulling himself heavily to his paws with the aid of the walking stick he always carried. "He's nocht but trouble. I dinna ken what he does with all his time and I dinna care, but he's up to nae guid. You mark my words. There's mischief afoot or my name's nae Jock Colquhoun."

And he hobbled off down the path, grumbling to himself.

"But . . . ?" began Winston, anxious to find out more about the chief's nephew.

"Nae 'ifs and buts', mon," snapped Jock, clearly upset. "Ye'll have the misfortune o' meetin' him soon enough. Ye can judge for yerself."

Winston followed the old dog back through the maze into the castle. As quickly as he could, he galloped back to his room to tell Hound all that he had heard from Jock. But the bloodhound was not there.

"I have been on a walking tour of the island," he explained when he finally returned an hour or so later. "There is little to be seen save crofters' cottages and fishermen's huts. It is a bleak land, in fact, swept by the cruel Atlantic gales . . ."

"Hound . . ."

"Bracken and peat bogs cover the island, with the occasional tuft of heather for colour. I fancy it is difficult to earn a living from such bare soil . . ."

"Hound . . ."

"The natives are simple, friendly folk, mainly of the Scottish terrier line, although I did see a most interesting breed of dog, a huge fellow, even larger than the MacSporran . . ."

"Hound!" barked Winston, almost bursting with

his own news. "I've got so much to tell you . . ."

"*You* have?" drawled Hound, raising his eyebrows . . . almost.

"Yes, Hound," cried Winston. And he poured out all that old Jock had told him about the MacSporran curse.

The bloodhound listened carefully, asking the occasional question. He smiled when Winston came to the part about the pipe-playing ghost.

"I'm sure you are aware that my work has always been based on the scientific," he said, leaning back in his chair and arching his paws. "There is always a natural reason for a supernatural act. Indeed, in my opinion . . ." But he was interrupted by a loud metallic booming in the distance.

"Thunder!" exclaimed Winston, his whiskers twitching in alarm. "Oh, I hate thunder."

"Nonsense," chided Hound. "It is merely the dinner gong summoning us to the dining room. If we set out immediately," he smiled, "we should get there before the meal is quite finished."

The MacSporran was waiting for them at the door of the dining room. He was magnificently dressed in full Highland rig from his buckled shoes to the ruffle of fine lace at his throat.

He welcomed them warmly and introduced them to his "very dear friend" Ian MacTavish.

The MacTavish was an old dog, even older than Jock Colquhoun, with an impish look in his beady little eyes.

"Ian is our historian," explained the chief, putting a paw affectionately around the old dog's shoulder. "If there's anything at all you want to know about these islands, Ian's your man."

"It would give me great pleasure to talk with you, Sir," said Hound. "Indeed . . ." He stopped in mid-sentence and stared past Ian MacTavish as if he had just seen the castle ghost. Winston fearfully peered over his own shoulder to see what had caught Hound's attention. In the doorway of the dining hall stood a large dog, a Scottish deerhound of the same family as the MacSporran. But there the resemblance ended.

He wore a brilliant kilt of deep red and blue with matching stockings. Over a full-sleeved white satin blouse, he wore a blue velvet coat and waistcoat, both richly ornamented with gold lace and embroidery. Gaily coloured ribbons sprouted from his shoulders and wrists. His shoes were of black kid, with red heels and white bows, his paws covered with magnificent rings.

When he was quite sure he had the attention of everyone in the room, he swept them all a deep bow.

The MacSporran introduced him as his nephew Finlay.

"Sherlock Hound!" exclaimed Finlay in a high pitched, rather squeaky voice. "Not the famous detective . . . ?"

"None other, Sir," agreed Hound.

"And what brings you to my . . ." Finlay

corrected himself quickly, "to *our* little island? Surely there is no crime here for you to solve?"

"Indeed no," answered Hound, smiling. "I am here purely for pleasure, to inspect your uncle's superb collection of clarsachs."

"Ah, the clarsach!" gushed Finlay. "An exquisite instrument. I will play it for you after dinner."

"That would indeed be a pleasure," said Hound.

"Did you have an enjoyable afternoon, Dr Winston?" said the MacSporran, turning to the sheepdog who was trying not to stare at Finlay's gaudy clothes and affected manners.

"I certainly did," he said. "I got lost . . . I mean, I walked around your maze."

"A maze?" said Hound, amazed.

"Ay," said Ian MacTavish, taking up the conversation. "It was planted by one o' the MacSporran's granddaddies, a foolish mon who followed all the fashions, guid or bad. All the Sassenach lords had a maze, so the auld MacSporran had to have one too. It was built in the lea of the castle, protected from the fiercer winds from the Atlantic Ocean, but it's nae easy to grow anything in this barren land."

"*We* had a maze," piped up Finlay.

"Where?" snapped the MacTavish.

"On my father's estate."

"Estate?" barked the old dog, curling his lip with scorn. "Your daddie had a parcel o' land nae bigger than my right paw. There was barely room for one small tree on it, let alone a maze."

Finlay pouted and went red with rage.

"And how was *your* afternoon, Mr Hound?" said the MacSporran quickly, anxious to avoid a dog fight between his nephew and MacTavish.

"Most interesting," drawled Hound. "I went for a long walk and had the good fortune to meet some of the islanders."

"They're a fine people," said the MacSporran, "but there are few of them left now. All the young lads and lassies leave for the mainland as soon as they grow up."

"What precisely is the population of this island?" enquired Hound.

The MacSporran looked at MacTavish.

"Aboot a hundred," said the old historian, "most o' them auld folk, shepherds or fishermen. It's hard to make a livin' on the Isle of Bogles."

"I did see a rather interesting breed of dog during the course of my walk," said Hound. "I suspect he was not an islander, although I did not have the opportunity of finding out."

"A huge laddie wi' a red coat and black beard?" enquired MacTavish.

"Just so," said Hound.

"Ay, that'll be one o' the O'Reillys."

"Ah yes, the O'Reilly brothers, two handsome young dogs who recently came here from Ireland," said the MacSporran.

Hound looked puzzled. "Why did they come here?" he said.

"Why? Because it is the most beautiful place in the whole world," said Ian MacTavish, as if it were perfectly obvious to anyone but a fool.

"Shall we sit down to dinner?" said the MacSporran, leading his guests towards the great candle-lit table in the centre of the room. "Mr Hound, perhaps you will sit on my right and Dr Winston on my left. Ian, please sit next to Dr Winston, and Finlay . . . Finlay?"

They all turned to look at the young dog, who seemed to be having some difficulty getting his rump down on the chair without sitting on the point of his sword.

"Ye'd better take it off, laddie," advised MacTavish, watching Finlay twist and turn, "or ye'll do yerself a terrible mischief."

"I assure you I am quite used to coping with a sword," said Finlay, getting redder and redder in the face.

"Will you try some of our heather ale?" said the MacSporran to Hound and Winston. "It is a potent brew made of heather-bells, honey and ginger." He poured a little in their glasses and raised his own in a toast "To our visitors from . . ." he began, but was rudely interrupted by Finlay who, giving up the attempt to sit down, suddenly flung back his chair, sprang upon it and placed one paw unsteadily on the table.

"No, no! We must have a toast in the Gaelic!"

he squeaked, raising his glass and wobbling dangerously on the overturned chair.

"*Suas e, suas e, suas e!*" he began, in a ringing voice.

"Have a care wi' yon sword," growled MacTavish. "Ye've nearly poked my eye out twice."

"Tch! Please!" muttered the young dog, annoyed at the interruption. "*Suas e, suas e, suas e!*" he began again.

"Cheers!" said Winston, and started to drink.

"I've not finished yet!" exclaimed Finlay, glaring at him.

"Oh dear, I'm so sorry." Winston put down his glass in a state of acute embarrassment.

"*Suas e, suas e, suas e!*" intoned Finlay for a third time. "*Sios e, sios e, sios! A null e, a nu . . .*"

A loud groan of agony rang out.

Finlay turned on MacTavish in a fury. "Have you no respect for tradition?" he shrieked. "This is a toast our forefathers made back in the mists of time!"

"It wasna me, laddie," protested the old dog.

Finlay cleared his throat and began again.

"*A null e, a null e, a null e!*" he wailed. "*Na h-uile . . .*"

Again a long, loud groan stopped him dead. It seemed to echo round the castle, rebounding off the old dark walls.

The MacSporran turned white.

"MacTavish!" squealed Finlay, quite beside

himself with anger now. "I'll give you one more chance . . ."

"I've already told ye, laddie, it wasna me," insisted the old dog.

Finlay raised his glass again, keeping a close eye on MacTavish.

"*Na h-uile ta gu math duit, a char* . . ." he chanted.

For the third time a groan rang out, longer and louder than before. And then, faintly at first but growing stronger every minute, came the sound of the dreaded ghostly bagpipes.

Finlay froze to the spot, his glass raised in the toast but no sound coming from his open mouth.

Nearer and nearer drew the fearful pipes.

The only other sound in the whole castle was the knocking of Winston's knees.

Suddenly Finlay let out a howl of terror. "It's the ghost!" he yelped. "It's the phantom piper . . . he's coming! He's coming!" And, scrambling down from his perch, he bounded out of the room, his tail between his legs, his ears flattened.

Hound rose quickly and made to follow him but was instantly prevented from doing so by the MacSporran's firm paw on his shoulder.

"Stay and enjoy your dinner, my friend," he insisted.

"But the g . . . g . . . the g . . . g . . . ?" protested Winston, from under the table.

"The ghost will not harm you," said the MacSporran in a quiet voice. "The business he has to conduct is between him and me. And now, let us raise our glasses in a simpler Gaelic toast than the one my nephew was attempting. *Slainte!*"

The others raised their glasses in response. Winston, under the table, raised his, but it rattled loudly against his teeth.

Somewhere deep in the bowels of the castle, the bagpipes droned on.

"I have a special treat for you," said the MacSporran, as a servant entered carrying a huge silver tray, "haggis."

"Haggis? Oh no!" groaned Winston. A haggis and a ghost were just too much for one night.

Despite his protests, Winston's plate was heaped high with the spicy meat and he made a polite attempt to eat it. The pipes seemed to be growing fainter, to his relief, and the MacSporran chatted casually as if nothing out of the ordinary had happened.

As the meal drew to a close, he turned to his guests with a smile and suggested they might like to see some of the MacSporran heirlooms.

Hound agreed readily and the whole party trotted out of the dining room and up a winding staircase until they came to a heavily barred door.

"Some of these jewels have been in my family for hundreds of years," said the MacSporran, unlocking the door and putting down the candlestick. "Please feel free to examine them yourselves."

Winston stepped into the room and gasped. It was like an Aladdin's treasure cave, filled to the brim with gold and silver, pearls and pewter, and emeralds and sapphires which glinted brilliantly in the candlelight.

Hound was lost in admiration too, picking up a small silver dagger, its handle encrusted with rubies, pausing to examine a solid gold shield, exclaiming over a snuff box inlaid with mother of pearl, an exquisite cameo or an opal ring.

The MacSporran patiently explained the historical background of every gem, on which Hound questioned him eagerly, but his heart was not in it. The sad, haunted look had come back to his eyes and, despite himself, he was listening all the while to the faint, eerie sound of the phantom pipes.

"Forgive me, gentlemen," he apologised after a while. "I regret that I am not in good spirits this evening but it has been a long and tiring day," he said, leading them back to the main hall.

"For us too," agreed Winston, stifling a yawn.

"Here, take this," said the MacSporran, giving Hound a candlestick, "it will light you back to your room."

Hound and Winston took leave of the chief and MacTavish and headed back to the quarters for distinguished guests, Hound leading the way.

Of Finlay there was no sight or sound.

The piping ghost seemed to have paused for a breather, but Winston stayed close to Hound, so close that he frequently trod on the other dog's paws.

The castle was cold and creepy. A light wind moaned around the battlements and owls hooted mockingly as the two dogs crept by. Hound's candle made weird and terrifying shapes on the stone walls and bats flitted constantly above their heads.

Winston sighed with relief when they finally reached their room. He shut the door and locked and bolted it very carefully.

"Ghosts can get through locked doors, you know," said Hound, watching Winston's performance with amusement.

Winston turned white. "Oh dear," he said, "I had quite forgotten that."

"I suggest you put the subject out of your mind," said the bloodhound, drawing on his nightshirt and matching nightcap. "Ghosts are merely a product of the imagination."

"I hope you're right," muttered Winston, jumping quickly into bed and burying his head under the blankets. "Good night, Hound."

"Good night, old fellow."

In a few minutes the distinguished guests' quarters at Castle Bogle echoed with loud snores.

Some time later that night, however, Winston woke with a start. For one moment he quite forgot where he was, and then it all came back to him in a sickening rush: he was lying in a huge, canopied bed in a musty old room in an isolated tower in a haunted castle on a bleak island in the Atlantic Ocean.

And to make it worse, there were soft shuffling sounds outside his door.

He sat bolt upright, his hackles raised.

To his horror, the bedroom door began to open slowly and a shrouded figure entered and glided noiselessly towards the bed.

The sheepdog tried to cry out, but no sound came.

"Winston," whispered the figure urgently, coming to a halt beside the bed and leaning over him. "Winston, are you awake?"

For one terrible moment, Winston thought his heart had stopped beating. He could feel the ghost's icy breath on his face; he could smell the stale horror of the grave.

"Y . . . y . . . you . . . you know my name?" he managed to stammer.

"Don't be stupid, my good dog!" barked the phantom, in a familiarly irritable voice. "Since we have been living together for the past twenty years, I fancy I ought to know your name by now."

A candle flame flared and Hound's face appeared above it. "What's the matter with you?" he demanded. "You look as if you'd seen a ghost."

"I thought you were one," admitted the sheepdog, sheepishly. "Where have you been?"

"Oh, just conducting a little tour of the castle," said Hound airily, walking over to the window and looking out.

"At this time of night?"

"And why not?" retorted the bloodhound. "When people are all asleep, it is an excellent time to look around and . . . hullo!" he stopped abruptly.

"What is it?" said Winston, springing out of bed and joining Hound at the window. "What have you seen?"

"Look there!" Hound pointed. "Do you see what I see?"

Winston peered as hard as he could but the great mass of hair over his eyes prevented him from seeing anything that wasn't right under his nose.

"I don't know," he confessed. "Tell me what you see and I'll tell you if I can see it too."

"Oh really!" grunted Hound irritably. "There is a figure in a white satin blouse and multi-coloured kilt, flitting from bush to bush in a very suspicious manner."

"A white satin blouse and a multi-coloured kilt . . . why, that must be Finlay!" exclaimed Winston in excitement.

"Indeed it must," agreed Hound. "Finlay MacSporran, creeping stealthily through the castle grounds in the dead of night. Now I wonder what that young pup is up to," he said, rubbing his snout thoughtfully, "I wonder."

4

A Blether wi' MacTavish

The next morning Hound decided to pay Ian MacTavish a visit. The MacSporran had not joined them for breakfast, old Jock explaining that the chief was "a wee bit sick."

Finlay was not at the breakfast table either.

"No doubt he is tired after last night's outing," said Hound quietly to Winston.

Ian MacTavish lived in a lovely old stone house set in a forest clearing at the foot of a hill a mile or so from Castle Bogle.

He greeted Hound and Winston warmly and invited them into his parlour for a "wee spot o' tea" and a piece of home-made shortbread. Inside, the house was a jumble of books and documents and old parchments.

"Just clear them all to one side, laddie," said MacTavish to Winston, who was wondering where to sit, since every armchair and settee was covered with books and papers of one sort or another.

"Ye've come to blether aboot the MacSporran, nae doot," said the old historian when they were all comfortably seated and sipping hot, sweet tea.

"Well, uhm, not really. I had in mind more of a social visit," protested Hound, who disliked his motives to be so readily uncovered.

"Dinna fool wi' me, mon," chuckled MacTavish, "I have the second sight, ye know."

"Second sight?" echoed Winston, intrigued. "Does that mean you wear bifocals?"

"It means that our good friend has the ability to read people's minds," said Hound. "Although I doubt it would take him more than a second to read yours from cover to cover," he added.

"I can see into the future too," added the Scot.

"Oh good," Winston turned his paws over and extended them towards MacTavish. "I wonder if you'd tell my fortu . . ."

"Not now!" snapped Hound irritably.

"What is it ye want to blether aboot?" said MacTavish, turning to the bloodhound.

"I am very interested in history," confided Hound, "and I was hoping that you might have in your possession the MacSporran family tree."

"Indeed I do, laddie," said MacTavish, getting to his paws and rummaging among a pile of dusty old parchments in a bookcase. "I have it here somewhere," he added, throwing pieces of paper in all directions. "Ah," he exclaimed at last, "here it is."

Hound seized the parchment greedily.

"It's near a hundred years old," said MacTavish, as Hound unrolled the great scroll. "Ye

can barely read the writin', the ink's sa faded."

Hound produced his glass and pored over the parchment in rapt concentration.

"It goes back to the fourth century, I see," he said, his tail twitching with excitement. "What a fascinating document. Truly fascinating." He ran his paws down the long list of ancient names. "Magnus, Sigtryg, Lagman, Ranald . . ." he mumbled, "Eoin, Allan, Torquil . . . ah!" Suddenly he let out an exclamation of delight. "Splendid!" he said, more to himself than the other two. "Quite splendid."

"What did you find, Hound?" asked Winston, peering at the faded letters in his usual blind way.

"Oh, nothing special," answered Hound airily, straightening up and walking back to his chair as if he were no longer remotely interested. "I was just checking on the MacSporran's ancestry."

"Ay, it goes way, way back," said MacTavish. "The MacSporran springs from a lang, lang line o' brave warriors. More's the pity it should end up wi' a blethering idiot like young Finlay."

"He's not the chief, yet," said Hound smoothly.

"Nay, but he will be," sighed MacTavish. "Ye know aboot the curse, I presume?"

Hound nodded. "I put no store by ghosts and curses," he said drily.

"Mebbe not," said MacTavish, "but the MacSporran does. He's seen all his granddaddies keel over and die when the phantom piper plays his awful tune."

"It is awful," agreed Winston, wincing at the memory.

"I was usin' awful in the correct sense o' the word, laddie, which means awe inspiring," explained the learned Scot. "Although I must agree the way yon wee ghostie plays the pipes is a sore torment to the ears and I canna blame the MacSporran's great-great-great-great-great-granddaddy for puttin' an end to it."

"The MacSporran was to be married soon, I understand," said Hound.

"Ay, that he was. The wedding was to take place in July and we were all as happy as larks when he told us."

"When was that, pray?"

"Aboot the end of May."

"That would be four weeks ago," Hound nodded. "And when did Finlay arrive?"

"On a cold, dark day in February," said MacTavish. "I remember it weel. We'd had a good winter, nae storms nor gales and hardly any snow. I was out walkin' one mornin' and I met the MacSporran wi' a worried look in his eye. 'Ian,' he said. 'I've some sad news. My only brother is dead and his son, Finlay, is comin' to live wi' me at the castle.' Weel, that was bad news but I didna realise how bad until I saw the laddie hisself. The day he arrived the weather changed for the worse. We had thirty inches o' snow and a gale that swept roofs off."

"Well, I thank you for the delicious refreshment and the information," said Hound, rising to his paws. "And now we must be on our way. I am rather interested in meeting some of the other residents of this island," he paused, "the O'Reilly brothers, for example."

"Ay, they're a grand couple," agreed MacTavish. "Gentlemen to the tips o' their whiskers. But ye'll nae meet both o' them today."

"Oh?" Hound attempted to raise his eyebrows but the heavy folds of skin hanging over his eyes made it impossible.

"Sean O'Reilly is here but his brother Finnegan is back in Ireland, attendin' to family business, so I'm told."

"What a pity," said Hound, "I should have liked to meet both of them. How long has Finnegan been away, do you know?"

"Weel, he left . . . let me see now, when did he leave?" The Scot scratched his head. "It was a few weeks back. Ay, I remember now . . . he left a day or so after the MacSporran announced his engagement to wee Jeanie Kilgallen. But he won't be back for some time, so his brother says."

At the door Hound turned suddenly and snapped his claws. "Dear me," he said, in an exasperated way. "I had quite forgotten to inform my brother Shylock of my safe arrival. Do you suppose one of the lobster fishermen would carry a letter to the mainland for me?"

"Ay, he would," said MacTavish, "if ye put a gold sovereign in his paw first. Gae doon to the harbour and tell wee Willie I sent ye. Ye'll be needin' a sheet o' paper and a pen, I suppose?"

"If I might trouble you."

"Och, it's nae trooble at all, mon," said the old historian, diving into a bureau and searching furiously for several minutes.

"Will this do?" he asked, finally emerging with a rather dog-eared piece of paper.

"Admirably," said Hound, taking up a pen and writing a few words on the sheet, which he then put in an envelope and sealed. "Good day to you, Mr MacTavish."

"And to ye," said the Scot, seeing them off at the door. "Ye'll come again?"

"We shall, indeed."

Wee Willie was doubtful about making the boat trip to the mainland because there was, he said, a cruel wind blowing from the west, but Willie's mind and the cruel wind suddenly changed direction when he saw the glint of gold in Hound's outstretched paw.

"You will deliver it personally to Shylock Hound, my good man?" insisted the detective.

"Ay, that I will," replied the crusty old fisherman, testing the sovereign with his teeth.

"Well, that's done," said Hound with satisfaction, as Willie clambered into his boat and rowed away. "And now for a pleasant walk back over the hills to the castle. We should be just in time for lunch . . . Ah!" he turned to Winston. "Unless I'm mistaken, that splendid figure of a dog striding towards us is Sean O'Reilly himself."

As the three dogs drew level, the Irishman touched his bonnet. "The top o' the mornin' to you," he said. "Sherlock Hound, isn't it? And Dr Winston. Sure and it's an honour to welcome you to our island."

"Has the news of our arrival spread already?" said Hound.

The Irish wolfhound put back his huge head and let out a roar of laughter.

"There's no keeping a secret here, begorrah!" he guffawed. "These folk know what you're thinking before you've even thought it!"

While Hound and O'Reilly chatted, Winston studied the Irishman with interest. He was the biggest dog Winston had ever seen, a huge, muscular animal with a commanding appearance and yet he seemed to be a friendly fellow, laughing and joking as if he had known them for years.

Eventually Hound said goodbye, promising to visit O'Reilly as soon as he possibly could, and he and Winston trotted quickly back to the castle.

Old Jock met them at the door with a long, mournful face.

"It's the chief," he said, in answer to Hound's questioning look, "he's dead."

"The curse . . ." whispered Winston in horror.

"How did it happen?" enquired Hound, who was more interested in facts than fantasy.

"The poor laddie was sick this morning," explained Jock. "Sa sick he couldna touch his

porridge. 'I've nae heart for it, mon,' he said wi' a sorrowful face, 'for I ken I'm goin' to die today.' Then he got out of his bed and said he would go fishin'. The chief aye loved to fish and I helped him push his boat oot and watched him row oot o' sight. I didna think more on it until lunch time and the MacSporran hadna come back. So I took some o' the young laddies and we rowed oot to sea to look for him. There was his boat, sure enough, bobbin' on the water . . . but nae MacSporran."

"Were there any signs of him?" asked Hound.

"Ay there were. The poor laddie's bonnet floatin' nearby, with its three wee feathers all wet and droopin'."

"How ghastly!" exclaimed Winston.

"It is a sad, sad loss to us all," agreed Jock, wiping a tear from his cheek.

"Have you broken the news to his nephew?" said Hound, who had a very practical nature.

"I have. And the laddie doesn't know whether to laugh, because he's now the chief, or weep, because he's lost a guid, kind uncle, the only relative he had left in the whole wide world."

"There is room for doubt on that point," said Hound quietly, following the old dog into the castle. "When will the funeral be?" he enquired.

"A week frae today," said Jock. "The body will lie in state in the great hall for the islanders to come and pay their last respects."

"But how can they pay respects to a body if

the body isn't there?" asked Winston, a little hesitant to mention such a painful subject.

"Ay, I hadna thought o' that," said Jock, scratching his ear in perplexity. "Weel," he decided, "we'll put oot the casket wi' nothin' in it. The MacSporrans have ay laid in state in the great hall and I dinna want yon chief to come back and haunt me because I didna do the right thing by him."

"Indeed no," agreed Winston, shuddering at the thought. "There are already quite enough ghosts around here as it is."

The castle was full of gloom, the servants wandering around in a daze, many of them weeping and wailing.

"I suppose we cannot decently leave until the funeral is over, can we?" said Winston hopefully later that day, watching great rain drops glide down the window.

"Certainly not!" snapped Hound. "It would be very ill-mannered, a sign of poor breeding on our part."

Winston sighed. "It's going to be such a long, long week," he said, "with simply nothing to do."

5

The Phantom Piper

The night of the MacSporran's death, the castle was quiet. The ghost had apparently achieved its purpose and gone away. Nobody was more relieved than Winston . . . unless it was Finlay, who was decidedly jolly the following morning.

"Thank goodness the piper has gone," said Winston, meeting Jock in the library some time later.

"He'll be back," grunted the old servant.

"But surely not for a long while," protested Winston.

"Dinna be sa sure, mon," said the other dog darkly. "There's only one MacSporran left now, and then the piper's work is all done."

Old Jock was right. That very night, as Winston was drifting off into sleep, the dreaded sound of the phantom pipes started up again, a long, desolate whine that foretold another tragedy for the MacSporran clan.

"Hound, wake up!" said Winston urgently, poking the bloodhound. "Wake up!"

"My dear fellow," came the reply, "I find I

have no choice since you are fracturing my rib cage with your elbow."

"But don't you hear it?" demanded Winston, beside himself with anxiety. "It's the . . . it's the piper."

"It is indeed the piper," agreed Hound. "But since your name is not MacSporran, you have nothing to fear from him. I suggest, therefore, that you go back to sleep . . . and permit me to do likewise," he added, pulling the blanket over his ears.

"But . . . but aren't you going to do anything about it?" demanded Winston, who was quite amazed at his friend's attitude. "I mean, don't you think you should . . . er . . . we should . . . ?"

A loud snore was his only answer.

Winston sank back on to his pillow, and listened to the ghostly pipes for a long while. At last he fell into a troubled sleep, full of hideous nightmares. Several times he woke with a start and a cry of fear, but Hound slept the sleep of the dead, snoring contentedly on his side of the bed.

Finlay was a nervous wreck at breakfast the next morning. His paws shook so much he dropped porridge down his sporran and knocked over the milk jug.

"I'm going away! I'm going away!" he squealed hysterically, heaping spoonfuls of salt into his tea cup in his agitation. "I'm not staying here to be hounded to death."

"It's nae use, laddie," said old Jock dourly.

"There's nae escape from the terrible fate that awaits ye."

"But there must be! There must be!" shrilled the doomed animal. "Mr Hound," he turned to the bloodhound beseechingly, "surely you can do something? You're the greatest detective in the whole world . . ."

Hound only smiled and shook his head. "I regret that even my incredible powers do not extend to to the realm of ghosts," he said smoothly.

"But I thought you didn't believe in them?" muttered Winston.

Hound shrugged. "You are quite correct, old fellow," he agreed. "I did not believe in them. But some of the inexplicable happenings that have occurred in this castle of late have persuaded me to change my mind."

Winston slumped back in his chair, a dejected look on his face. Hound had changed during the past few days. He seemed unaffected by the tragedy swirling around him, and Winston had never, never heard him describe any happening as inexplicable. Indeed, it was Hound's greatest boast that he could explain anything in reasonable, natural terms.

"It must be the air here," muttered Winston to himself as he plodded miserably round the castle grounds. "It's obviously not good for him." He pulled up his collar against the cold, damp breeze blowing from the sea. "It's not good for me, either," he added bitterly, wishing he and Hound were back in their comfortable rooms in London.

Winston was hurt, too, at the way his old friend had so readily abandoned him in favour of the new chief of the MacSporrans.

Hound and Finlay went for walks together or shut themselves up in the music room for hours at a time, twanging away at the Scottish harp or toasting their rumps before the great log fire in Finlay's private drawing room.

Poor Winston wandered around like a lost soul. He tried to chat with Jock, but the old servant was too grief stricken at the death of his master to engage in idle chatter. He went over the hill to visit Ian MacTavish but the house was always dark and deserted and nobody answered his persistent knocks. Once he was sure he saw a light in the living room, but it went out as he approached. Another time he thought he saw a dog at the rear of the house, but it quickly disappeared when Winston hollered.

And to make things worse, the ghost was back with a vengeance. Night after night the wail of the bagpipes resounded through the castle, coupled with loud groans of anguish and the clanking of heavy chains. Several times Winston distinctly heard the name "Finlay" echoing down the long, dark corridors as if the ghostly piper were calling the unhappy animal to his death.

"Just one more night," said Winston to himself the evening before the MacSporran's funeral, "just one more night in this terrible place."

He and Hound dressed for dinner and went down to the candlelit dining room. To Winston's surprise, Ian MacTavish was there, and Sean O'Reilly, the Irish wolfhound.

"Sure and it's a pleasure to see you again, Dr Winston," said the Irishman, shaking him firmly by the paw. "I've had many a long chat with your good friend Hound," he said, patting the detective on the shoulder in a very familiar fashion, "but I've seen nothing of you, more's the pity."

Winston's mouth fell open in surprise. "You've seen Hound . . . ?" he began.

"Er . . . yes, I have had the opportunity of meeting this gentleman on a number of occasions," said the bloodhound quickly, "although I forgot to mention it to you."

Again Winston was hurt. Hound seemed to be shutting him out of all his activities as if their old friendship stood for nothing.

"Shall we dine?" said Finlay, in a faint voice. The poor animal seemed completely dispirited. The nightly hauntings were obviously taking their toll of him. His paws shook and his eyes shifted constantly as if he expected someone or something to pounce on him out of the dark shadows. The gay, gaudy costumes he loved to wear had given way to the dullest of plaids. His face was unshaven, his sleeves unbuttoned and his shoes on the wrong paws. All in all he was a sorry figure of a dog.

The guests took their places at the dinner table, Winston facing O'Reilly, with Finlay at the head of the table.

The Irishman was in splendid spirits, cracking jokes and telling stories about his native Ireland. Despite the sadness hanging over them, Winston felt his own spirits beginning to rise, though whether that was because of O'Reilly's jokes or the heather ale, he couldn't say.

After a while Finlay too seemed to shake off his sombre mood and join in the laughter. Finally, as the meal drew to a close, he stood up. "Well, gentlemen," he said. "Shall we . . . ?"

But they never heard the question, for at that very moment the ghostly pipes started up in the distance.

"Oh no," groaned Finlay, sinking to his knees. "Oh no!"

"What a terrible row to be sure!" protested Sean O'Reilly, watching Finlay with keen interest.

"Terrible," agreed MacTavish, covering his ears. "I've never heard him play as badly as tonight. The poor wee ghostie must have indigestion."

"It's getting n . . . n . . . nearer," stammered Winston, preparing to dive under the table.

"Ay, that it is, laddie," agreed MacTavish in a hushed voice. "It's coming this way."

"Oooooooooooooooooooooooooh!" Finlay let out a great cry of anguish and leapt to his paws as if he were about to run away, but Hound slapped a firm paw on his shoulder and pressed him back into his seat.

"Stay where you are," he commanded grimly. "Don't move from that chair whatever happens."

For one moment, Winston recognised the old authoritative Hound . . . and he was glad.

Closer and closer came the pipes, and the happy-go-lucky smile on O'Reilly's face turned into a frown.

"What's he doing?" he muttered to himself once or twice. "Sure and he's playing the fool tonight."

The rest of the group waited in horrified silence as the ghostly pipes drew nearer and nearer.

Suddenly Finlay let out a howl of terror and pointed to the door. "He's here! He's here! He's come to get me!" And he sprang up, sending his chair crashing to the floor.

"What the . . . ?" Winston exclaimed in amazement as a huge Irish wolfhound came through the door playing the bagpipes, followed closely by a bloodhound pointing a gun at the piper's head.

O'Reilly took one look and leapt for the window.

"Get him!" barked the bloodhound. And MacTavish quickly drew a gun.

"Dinna move, laddie," he commanded, "or I'll blow the brains right out o' your head."

O'Reilly cowered in a corner, covered by MacTavish's gun.

"Good evening, Winston," said the bloodhound, still keeping his own gun pointed at the piper.

"Hound!" cried Winston. "Then who is this . . . ?" he said, pointing to the bloodhound sitting opposite him at the dining table.

Suddenly the penny dropped.

"Why, you're Shylock!" he exclaimed.

"Indeed it is, old fellow," said Hound, prodding the Irish wolfhound into the room with his gun. "My brother Shylock has been standing in for me, so to speak, while I hunted the castle ghost. And I've caught him . . ."

"But I don't understand," whined Finlay, who was quite overcome by the whole thing and still shaking from top to tail.

"Elementary, my dear fellow," said Hound. "This 'ghostly piper' is Finnegan O'Reilly, as I'm sure you know. What you don't know, however, is that he is a distant relative of yours. A study of the MacSporran family tree will show you that your ancestors and the O'Reillys were related way, way back. Now do you understand?"

Finlay shook his head.

"Well, it is really quite simple," said Hound patiently. "The O'Reillys discovered the relationship a year or so ago. They also discovered that there were only two MacSporrans left, you and your uncle, and that both of you lay under a family curse. Now, the O'Reillys don't believe in ghosts, any more than I do, but if you cannot have a real ghost, you make one of your own. Now do you understand?"

Again Finlay shook his head.

Hound pointed to the wolfhound standing before him. "Finnegan here got into the castle and hid himself. At night he prowled around playing the bagpipes . . ."

". . . And frightened my poor master to his death," added Jock, who had come into the room to see what all the noise was about. "Just let me get my paws on him," said the devoted servant, glaring at the great dog towering over him. "I'll . . . I'll . . ."

"No you won't, Jock. Not before I do," said a voice behind him.

Jock spun round and let out a howl of joy. "It's the MacSporran!" he exclaimed, tears of joy brimming in his eyes.

"Uncle!" exclaimed Finlay, "You're alive! But I thought you were in the coffin in the hall . . . I mean, at the bottom of the sea."

"No, I'm not, laddie," said the MacSporran, coming into the room. "I'm alive and well . . . thanks to Sherlock Hound."

6

All is Revealed

"But if your brother Shylock was with me at the castle all the time, Hound," said Winston later that evening, when both the O'Reillys were safely locked in the castle dungeon, "then where were you?"

Hound pointed to Ian MacTavish. "Staying with this gentleman," he said. "As, indeed, was the MacSporran. We were both, one might say, concealed under one roof."

"So that's why you wouldn't open the door to me when I came to visit," said Winston, offended again that he had not been involved in the plot.

"I'm sorry, old fellow," apologised Hound, "but it was vital that you thought I was still at the castle. If you had known otherwise, you might not have acted convincingly and certain other people might have smelled a rat."

"The O'Reillys, you mean?"

"The O'Reillys, of course, and Finlay."

"You suspected me?" squeaked Finlay, who was still suffering from shock after all that had happened.

"In a case such as this, everyone is suspect," replied Hound, in his usual cool manner, "and I would have been foolish had I overlooked the obvious fact that you stood to gain a great deal by getting rid of your uncle before he married and produced a son and heir."

"But what made you suspect the O'Reillys, Mr Hound?" said the MacSporran.

"From the moment I saw your family treasure," said Hound, "I knew the ghost must be a real, flesh and blood creature who was anxious to get his greedy paws on it. The O'Reillys interested me. Why would they leave their native Ireland to come to a . . . forgive me . . . to a rather bleak little blackwater in the Hebrides? I was also aware that there was some suggestion of Irish wolf-hounds and Scottish deerhounds being related and, by a stroke of good fortune, you have an excellent historian on the island who had the MacSporran family tree in his possession. A quick glance at it confirmed my suspicions. However," continued Hound, as his audience listened with rapt attention, "their guilt was finally confirmed as soon as I heard about the MacSporran's wedding."

"My wedding?" repeated the MacSporran, frowning.

"Indeed," said Hound. "The O'Reillys came to this island a little over a year ago, I understand. They were quite content to bide their time until the islanders accepted them, but the announcement of your intention to marry speeded up their plan of action. The day following your engagement party, if you remember, Finnegan disappeared. He had gone back to Ireland on family business, or so his brother said. A short time after that the hauntings began, am I not right?"

"Ay, ye are, laddie," agreed Jock, who was listening intently from his corner.

"On discovering this fact, I was quite sure of their guilt," said Hound. "It simply remained for me to discover where Finnegan O'Reilly was hiding and if your nephew Finlay was also involved in the plot."

The MacSporran's nephew pouted. He was just beginning to realise that his chances of inheriting the MacSporran title and treasure were fading fast . . . and he didn't like it at all.

"In order to find out whether Finlay was guilty or innocent," continued Hound, "I instructed the MacSporran to . . ." he chuckled noiselessly, "to have shall we say, an accident at sea, which he managed very convincingly, I think."

"Ay," agreed Jock, with feeling, "too convincingly."

"When the 'ghostly' piper returned after the MacSporran's apparent death, I knew that Finlay was innocent," said Hound. "I, therefore, set out to discover the ghost's true identity. This was made easier for me by my brother, who obligingly came in answer to my urgent letter and played the part of Sherlock Hound at the castle, a very quiet, inactive Sherlock Hound who would not give any criminals a moment's concern. In the meantime, I positioned myself outside the castle. Since nobody suspicious came or left, however, I presumed the 'ghost' was inside. But where? Real ghosts live on air . . . or so I would imagine . . . but flesh and blood imitations must eat. And so I hid near the castle kitchens and waited for my solid ghost to appear in the dead of night."

"Marvellous!" exclaimed the MacSporran. "Sherlock Hound, you are a genius."

"Oh, it was nothing." The detective dismissed the praise with a wave of his paw.

"But where was Finnegan O'Reilly hiding?" said Finlay.

"Come," Hound commanded them, rising to his paws. "I will show you." And he led them all out of the room, down a short passageway and into the castle library.

"Ha! Ha!" cried Jock. "It's one o' yon bookcases, nae doot. Ye press a button and the bookcase swings open, am I nae right?" he said, pleased as punch with himself.

"I'm afraid not," said Hound, walking to the great open fireplace. "But if you will press this flagstone, Jock, you will soon discover the answer."

Jock pressed one of the big grey stones and a door at the back of the fireplace silently swung open revealing a flight of stairs.

"Hoots, mon!" he exclaimed. "D'ye mean to say that's been there all these years and I never knew it?"

"Indeed it has," said Hound. "If you care to go up the stairs, you will find a small room at the top. I believe such rooms are called priests' holes. They make a perfect hiding place for a castle ghost."

The MacSporran went first, with Finlay, MacTavish and Jock following.

"I say, Hound," said Winston, drawing the detective to one side when the others had disappeared up the stairs, "did you ever discover what Finlay was doing in the castle grounds at night?"

"I did," whispered Hound with a smile. "He was off to visit a fisherman's daughter—a pretty young creature, but of decidedly low birth."

7

Auld Lang Syne

The MacSporran insisted they stay for his wedding.

"There'll be feasting and dancing," he said, dismissing Hound's mild protests. "And you will be the guest of honour," he added, "after my bride, of course."

Although Hound disliked social occasions, he felt obliged to stay. For his part, however, Dr Winston enjoyed himself hugely, doing a highland fling with the bride and kissing all the bridesmaids . . . twice. He was sorry when the time finally came to say goodbye to the MacSporran, Jock and MacTavish, and the leave-taking was a sad occasion.

"Ye'll come back," cried Jock, waving to them as the small boat pulled away from the shore. "Ye'll come back soon."

Then he and MacTavish and the MacSporran joined paws and sang "Auld Lang Syne", the sad refrain floating across the water until the boat was out of sight.

When the Hound brothers and Winston reached Kelpie Hall, Mrs MacDougall greeted them with cries of delight.

"Have ye got rid o' ye cold, laddie?" she demanded of Winston, looking at him in her usual motherly fashion.

The sheepdog nodded.

"Weel, I've a wee surprise for ye dinner tonight," she said, with a twinkle in her eye.

"Carrageen Jelly?" enquired Hound innocently.

Winston hastily put a paw to his mouth.

"Nae," said the old housekeeper. "This is something ye'll both enjoy . . . a dish frae your own country, a steak and kidney puddin'!" she ended triumphantly.

"A steak and kidney puddin', lassie!" exclaimed Winston in disgust. "I dinna want yon steak and kidney puddin'. Gi' me a guid haggis or a dish o' stovie tatties. I'll nae be eatin' yon Sassenach food."

Mrs MacDougall's mouth fell open.

"D'ye nae ken wha' I'm sayin', lassie?" persisted Winston.

"I think my old friend spent a little too much time with Jock Colquhon," said Hound quietly to his brother. "The poor fellow will never be understood in London. And, indeed," he added, "he shows no desire to return to London . . . a fact which causes me considerable concern since I am due to return there tomorrow for a very important engagement."

"Leave it to me," said Shylock with a sly wink. "I'll have him out of here in no time, you'll see. Dr Winston," he addressed the sheepdog in a loud voice, "would you care to stay with us at Kelpie Hall for a while longer?"

"Aye, mon, that I would," replied Winston warmly.

"Splendid," beamed Shylock. "You are most welcome to stay as long as you like. And now gentlemen, let us go into the dining room and sample Mrs MacDougall's excellent steak and kidney pudding. Incidentally, Dr Winston," he said, as they took their places at the dining table, "did I ever tell you what Kelpie means?"

The sheepdog shook his head.

"Ah, it is really quite interesting," continued Shylock, smiling. "It is the Gaelic word for a devil. Kelpie Hall was so named because it has been haunted by a terrifying demon for many centuries. I, myself, have seen it and a most fearful sight it is. Often I have been wakened in the middle of the night by horrible groans and . . . Dr Winston . . . ? Dr Winston . . . ?"

But the sheepdog was away, his case in his paw, loping down the road as fast as his short legs would carry him.

Folk who passed him on the way to the railway station heard him muttering under his breath:

"Frae witches, warlocks an' wurricoes
An' evil spirits and all things
That gang bump i' the night,
May the Guid Lord deliver us . . ."

Amen.